Mental Health Through the Written Word

Poetry

I want to give my thanks to my amazing support system- My family and friends. You are truly amazing, and I love you all. You know who you are.

It is okay to have not-so-okay days! -Charlotte

All in My Head

Please don't ignore me when I cry in your presence, for it took twelve months just to get the referral letter.

Please don't judge me or brand me with your stigma I could be your mother, aunt, sister or your brother.

You never saw the effort it took to just get from my bed just to face all the disappointing looks and to be told it's all in your head.

Mental Health Through the Written Word

Nan

Toast cut into triangles,
Toast with butter and jam.

Surrounding the TV,
Watching 'Bigfoot' for the 11th time,
Whilst you sat there knitting away,
The needles clicking ever so often.

You take us upstairs,
And you bathe us,
Towel at the ready in case we get soap in our eyes.
I was so lucky to have a nan like you.
You scraped our hair,
Always on the look-out for lice.

You go to your bedroom and pick up your old biscuit tin,
We head downstairs and we open it excitedly,
Knowing every time there will be no biscuits,
But Lego, living out its last days after all these years,
We play,
We create stories,
We laugh,
We make up characters,
And we become a team.

Whilst you're sitting there,
Reading a book,
In a state of dreams.

The smell of stale tobacco,
Mixed with your old perfume,
There is nothing left of you now,
You don't know us anymore,
You don't remember our triangle toast or our soapy baths.
You pass away, silently,
You move to another plane,
I can cope,
Just about,
Knowing you're my angel sparkling in the night sky,
I can feel you,
You are you,
You are sane,
You are the same,
You are my main,
Nan, be tame,

For your name sparkles with fame,
You're loved to the point of no return,
My ears burn,
As you talk of me in a way so stern.
Nan, I love you.
I love you and your triangular toast.

The care I require

The tears of frustration,
no justification,
No care.

This condition is REAL.
No 'hysteria' as what it was called before.
It is no longer a conversion disorder,
As that has outdated us all.
This is not a psychological issue.

It has moved on to functional neurological disorder,
A disorder where there is misfiring of the brain signals.
Now that is real.
The tremors, the jerks, the seizures,
They don't really bother me.
What bothers me is the fact they dismiss me,
But no matter how hard I try,
There will be challenges,
Yet I will arise.

My superhero

You're my superhero,
My inspiration,
My motive.

You gave me purpose to be fulfilled.

You deserve everything in the whole entire world,
And I cannot wait until I can truly give you everything.

But for now, love will have to do,
Love conquers all,
And today, I will shower you in love and all things nice.

I love you

The fool

Unblocking the impulse of the soul
Recklessness
Holding back
Time to wait
False start

The unblocking,
The unblocking of impulse,
Impulse of the soul.
This is what it is to be like,
To be a fool.
Acting recklessly,
Not thinking before you do,
This card urges you to hold back from go,
It is time to wait, You don't want a false start,

There are new beginnings and fresh starts,
Time to start over and start something new.
But you will never be able to start over,
And you will never be able to do something new,
Unless you take the leap of faith.
This is about finding yourself,
A journey of the soul,
You may act with innocence,
You may act with Impulse,
But you are merely just the fool.

The Magician

You make skilful uses of your energies,
You made do with what you have,
You use your time well.

You channel inspiration,
And you can manifest power,
But please don't forget that the willpower must come from you.

You have a creative discipline,
Creating magic and potions infinitely,
You are skilful but mostly known for your resourcefulness.

However, wisdom in reverse,
You have a blocked channel,
You need to be regaining your willpower and skill.
So that you can remove blockages to your manifestation.
You may feel disempowered, as you cannot put your skills to good use,
And so you use manipulation to feed your ego and your soul,
As you require the control to bring about your goal.

The High Priestess

Being the High Priestess means you have reached ultimate enlightenment,
You live through your life with a deep inner knowing and divine wisdom.
Your intuition tells you things you would never have known,
You know so much, your heart must be made of stone.
You have psychic abilities that go beyond of this earth,
Whether you're a clairvoyant or not,
You feel what others feel,
You think what others think,
You feel strongly,
But do you do what others do?
You have a sense of foresight,
With the use of your third eye.
You use your foresight to predict the future,
Not letting your past hold you back.
This card gives a sense of fertility, a sense of new life being brought into the world.

In a downright reverse,
You may be disconnected from intuition,
You have no idea what you're facing,
Or indeed what you are about to face.
You use your past lessons to predict the future, rather than relying on yourself.
Blockages to your intuition will need to be removed,
But that is near impossible,
When you're avoiding life.
You need to face up to the facts,
You need to face up to your fears,
You need to strength your intuition,
Growing deeper in your involvement with life itself.

Kicking Pain in the Ass

Crippled with fear,
I bow down to the Gods above me.

I beg,
I plead,
No more pain,
I can't take it anymore.

No more praying for drugs to help me,
No more days spent in bed.

Pain, you are utterly and completely derogatory.
You break me down into the smallest of pieces
You make me broken.

But I will rise above.

Throw away my broken parts and then,
I'm whole once again.

Allow me to live a whole other life,
A life where I can be me,
Without all this pain.

Eyes

My eyes are clear crystal marbles,
You will never see a tear shed.
I let you all think, I am on the mend,

But at night, the marbles disappear,
I swim in a flood of tears,
Holding the very own marbles that used to be mine,
Weighing me down,
Head under water.

It is sunrise, and my shiny marbles become part of me again,
Never letting you see a tear I may shed.

High

I hate that I had the temptation,
the urge to escape,
the sensation of leaving me high and dry.

Higher than a kite and drier than an empty wallet.

I might have enjoyed it, but it could have been horrific.
An altered state of reality.
A reality so horrific.

Is that the reality I am looking for?

Or can I just get high off life itself?
Can life give me what I am searching for?
Can life bring me the truest of joy?
An abundance of happiness I've been waiting for my entire life?

Morphine

A bottle of potion,
Magic fairy opiates,
A drug to take the pain away.
Severs the pain at both ends.

Allowing my brain to be washed over,
A blank canvas arising,
An hour or two to spend life with magical opiates swirling around in my blood.

Then it is back to a cold-hearted reality,
Where everything is black and white,
Tumble weed stumbling across my brain,
Completely lost for words,
And so, I take my magic fairy dust just to feel alive again.

Then, I realise I am an addict.
How can I think these magic fairy opiates will change my life?
How can I think they will make me better?
When all it does it mask the pain,
Both physical and emotional.

I drink the remainder of the magic opiate bottle and I decide,
I decided to be a recovering addict.

That was the day the addict kicked it,
And it clicked.
Clicked into place.
No morphine to make me better,
It is mind over matter,
To avoid addiction,
Avoiding addiction to avoid the affliction.
Avoiding the affliction of pain it causes everyone else.

Love is a piercing needle

Love is a piercing needle,
Slowly being pushed through the epidermis of your skin,
Inch by inch,
Burning as it grows deeper.

Love is what bites you in the ass,
As you love harder,
The knockbacks get stronger,
You once were resilient,
Now you are left as a sloppy heap on the floor.

You do not sob and you do not cry, as you allow them to walk past,
You silence and steady your breath,
You prepare yourself,
For the piercing needle,
Slowly being pushed through epidermis of your skin,
Inch by inch,
Burning as it grows deeper.

The bond becoming weaker,
The salt in the wound cools down your fever,
As you are left to be the preacher,
The preacher of love, independence and healing,
You allow your body to process the feeling.
Love is a piercing needle.

Pain is a leech

Pain is lurching,
Growing,
Expanding.

It never seems to go away,
Like when your shoes step in dog faeces,
It lingers and it sticks with you for the rest of the day.

It's like vaping clouds of severing pain,
Wandering about in the waves of clouds,
Not knowing what is next going to be on your pain scale.

Pain is the heartbreak you cause your family,
When all of a sudden you can't do the things you used to,
They just want to help,
They just want to take it all away.

Pain is mean.
It stings you with its tail at the most unexpected moment.

Pain is malicious
It intends to cause as much harm as possible.

Pain is your body,
It is the nerves in your body,
Alerting everyone else that something is wrong.
That something is broken.
That something may be me.

Pain is me.

Purpose

When the cold hair hits,
I suffer from condensation.
I suffer with leaky edges,
As rain trickles down to the edge
I can show a vague reflection when someone stands too close. I reflect light quicker than I reflect sound.
I am the opposite of opaque.
The sun light can scorch its way through and i can cause fires.
I have more purposes that you would think.

Yet you will still open me in the summer to make it warmer and brighter, you close at night to keep us warm and protected. You see I don't know what I am but I have many purposes and surely that is sufficient, is it not?

Sometimes I see life as so irrelevant,
So pointless,
Like, what really is the point?
Then I realise windows are so important,
So we must be at least as important as a window,
And that's what changed my mind set.

Mental Health Through the Written Word

I have never met you but…

I don't know you,
I have never met you
But maybe I will do,
One day.

You are the sweetest person,
I know that for certain.

You genuinely care
A problem halved is a problem shared,
And you don't seem to mind,
You're so kind.

I know pop vinyl's are your thing,
Collecting superheroes,
All as symbols,
Symbols of how strong you are,
Symbolising the very best you.

I want you to be comfortable,
Comfortable within yourself,
I want you to set yourself free,
Set yourself free and fly.
Fly higher than you could ever have imagined.

Cut me some slack

Cut me some slack,
It isn't my fault, the things I lack.
My pain is real, and that is a fact.

Yes, I do take strong medication,
But it keeps me afloat,
It enables me to complete my education.

So please, do not question my authentication,
I can offer you an explanation but I should not need to.

I am using all my will power,
All my determination,
To reach my destination.

I promise you I will never give up,
You will not be left a letter of resignation upon your desk,
because I am stronger and more dedicated than you think,

I am not giving up, by choosing to take medication,
There is so much repetition,
Are you not bored of your own voice yet?
Stop trying to put me in a box of man-made segregation,
You see I may have a disability,
And often my needs go through a process of delegation,
But do not let that affect my reputation.

Grievance

Tears are compulsory,
When a grievance occurs.

You told me not to cry when you are gone,
But please know I am not that strong.
I feel your soul in my playlists and songs.

A day will come,
Where I can take care of you again,
Where I can share my love with you once again.
Feeding my soul with music, songs and sound.

When I look up into the sky,
I visualise you looking over me,
Oh how I wish I could just offer you a cup of tea.
How I wish I could just set you free,
So there is more time for you and us three.

Dementia may have taken a hold,
Especially as you grew old.
Know that you make me want to fight your corner,
To help others with Dementia,
You make me bold.

Spotlight

Thousands of spotlights,
Circling each one of my steps,
I get funny looks,
And I hope one day the wind changes so their faces stay like that.
But In the meantime, I spend my life in a spotlight,
Each mark of my life critiqued and judged.
Comments are passed as I continue,
As I continue to await judgement day,

When will it come?

Expression

I fell in love with the expression; you can't fall in love at first sight,
It's a burning desire that grows deeper inside,
Developing over time,
Through dimension,
Through space.

It becomes a passion,
Something you want to write and talk about forever.

It can be unhealthy,
Why don't they like me in that way?
Am I not pretty enough?

But I have to stand back and accept,
Not everyone falls in love back.

<u>I have no right</u>

I have no right to love you,
But it's true, I love you too much.

I crave your gentle touch,
The pecks on my cheek,
The caressing of my skin.

Going back to all the places we have been,
Both mentally and physically,
I have no right to love you.
I have no right to need you,
But I still do,
I will happily wait in the queue.

I will never meet anyone else quite like you,
I know you love me,
Or at least I can pray that is true.

Yet, you still turned out to be the 'baddie'.

I beg you

I cry out in pain,
Having walked up the second flight of stairs,
I sit on your bed and cry,
Begging you to take the pain away.

But you judge me all wrong.
I can't go back there if I am like this, apparently.
How am I supposed to look after myself? You say,
You say I am addicted to pain killers,
But that isn't true,
Or is it?

I just want the pain to go away,
Go away and never come back,
For it to stop ruining my life,
For it to stop overtaking me,
Consuming me all of the time,
Dotting my skin with wet tears,
I beg for you to take the pain away.
There must be something you can do.
There must be something.
Anything.

My Father's Accomplishment

See,
I thought when it came to accomplishment,
It was about winning a football bet.
When I was young,
I thought being proud was being a part of a football team,
That overcoming was dribbling the ball past the defence.

But as I grew older,
And my writing became more prominent,
I realised many things.
I realised my daughter was my accomplishment,
And her accomplishment was overcoming her disability.

I found that love was reflected in her writing when she overcame disability,
When disability took her through the motions,
Her belief never faded,
Her belief in doing anything she wanted to do.

Adversity never stopped her.
Only for a brief moment, it would make things harder,
But that never put her ambitions to a halt.

That never stopped her writing.
That never stopped her believing, loving and being proud.
It never stopped her from loving football,
And it never stopped me from loving her.

Now I realise

And now I realise,
I realise what is good for me,
I realise what is bad for me,
I realise I need to keep myself safe.
Leaning on all of you,
I know you will help.
You will all help me get through this depression,
The depression that seemingly never ends,
The abyss,
It is time for it to stop now,
It is time for it to come to an end.

Manipulation

You made your point.
A point is what you made.
With those sharp needles,
Pricking into my heart,
And messing up my brain.

You had me thinking,
Just for a good second,
Am I good enough?
Can I do this?
Can I actually do this?
Can I make it?
Can I be the person I desire to be?

Screwed

I spent my life concentrating,
Concentrating on what I deemed to be so important,
Just for you to come and screw it all up by penetrating me.
By violating me.
By screwing with my body, you also screwed with my god damn mind.

I used to be that person that thought everyone was so kind,
As the tide comes in,
I was forced to realise I was wrong,
That people were not kind. That they screwed with you. They screwed with your mind.

That night,
You took a piece of me,
A piece I will never get back.
You took my power,
You took my control,
And you owned it.

Now it's my turn to reclaim that power and control.
So all I can do is turn around and say fuck you.

Sinful

I am so brave,
Won't let you cave me in,
I will be strong and devour the sin.

No Dismissal

The crashing waves rip through my body,
Causing it to tear,
Opening up my flesh wound,
Gauging at the fresh air,
Hitting with a cold reality,
This anxiety is not fair.

My chest is beating,
As fast as the 1600 bhp Hennesey twin turbo V,
It feels like the fastest in the world.

You see,
Anxiety is no joke.
You don't know if you're anxious, having a heart attack or a stroke.
Anxiety can be so severe that you can't work,
And people wonder why you're so broke.

Folks, I am here to say anxiety is no joke.

Aspire

I tried so hard,
Got so far,
From one transition,
To the next.

My bones shatter within in my body,
My eyes proceed to stream from the dust,
 I crawl,
I wriggle,
I squirm.

I picked myself up and I walked.
Why would I walk, if I wanted to fly?
My colours could be so radiant.
I know I could push myself further,
I could fly… if I really wanted to.
Such a restrictive cocoon,
It will be over soon.

 I pray my wings will unfold,
 To brush off the dust,
 To get stronger,
More resilient.
I stand tall,
I stretch my arms as wide as I can,
as I watch the beauty of my wings flourish,
so elegant and pure.
I am not against the odds anymore,
now that I have my wings. I can go even further.
I push myself,
and I eventually do things I had only ever dreamed of ever doing.

A Second Chance at Life

I crash and I burn,
I don't want to do this anymore.
I gave up,
I finished myself off,
In fact I didn't,
I fucking survived.
Against the odds,
With a breathing tube clawing away at my throat,
With a tube up my nose,
feeding me nutrition,
Why didn't I need the toilet?
I had a catheter in.
These three things saved me.
My housemate saved me.
71 saved me.
The paramedics saved me.
And I just don't remember.
All I wanted was to be finished off,
God didn't answer my prayers,
Maybe now is not the time to die.
Maybe my life is just starting.
Do I believe in fate?
After however many attempts, I do.
I am here to live,
I am here to survive.

The Unexpected

Didn't Expect that one,
Must've been keeping it quiet..

For she, the girl, has found the light ,
Under the moon of a starry night.
Her feet firmly on the grass,

The once, this girl, was tightened and gripped by chains,
But now that she is free,
The clock tower chimed,
As she realises,
She's finally quite sane, after all.

Insomnia

Lay me down,
Softly and gently,
Because I might just crumble into that of insanity.
Staring at a blank wall up above me,
Wondering when this will pass,
The loneliness felt inside,
The pain growing so strong.
The pain growing so fast,
I toss and I turn at night,
But I still cannot forget,
The damage has already had its impact,
And so I just let it come and torment me,
And then let it swallow me whole.

Then I have a revelation,
Although sleep will not happen,
I can happen.
I get out of bed and grab my art book and my crayons,
I draw and I shade until the night peacefully swallows me whole,
Insomnia will not take its toll.

Pills and Potions

I take these white pills,
Expecting a magic cure,
For all pain and suffering
To come to an end.
But it doesn't.
It never will.

And that's okay.

God

I feel sleepy,
Sleepy enough to go to sleep.
I wish I could sleep forever,
But God will not allow me to do so.

He forces me to push on,
He squeezes an ounce of strength into me so that I can walk again.

He strains me,
He pushes all of my buttons,
Just to see that I am still fighting,
Because he knows me,
God knows me well.

The testing of patience,
The testing of gratitude,
The testing of feeling unloved.

Yet I still push forward,
My days will commence.

Lost in Space

I am an alien,
An alien so alienated and trapped on earth.
Trapped by humans,
Humans that make me feel the things I don't want to feel anymore.
The love, the security,
It keeps me at bay.
Too scared to go back to my home planet
Home planet of depression and loneliness,
However, I have to look after the humans,
The ones that give me love and security and keep me at bay.

A Friend in Need

He is a jolly man,
He appreciates the small things,
And he knows you do too.

A cup of hot chocolate to help ease the pain,
Offering a helping hand,
To stop us from going mad.
He's a well good lad.

His positivity is very high, just a tad,
But yet that just leaves it difficult for us to be sad.

He appreciates his food,
He knows it can put us in a good mood
He will put on a classic tune,
And just very soon,
He will be out of here,
Out of the ward,
He will have learnt his boundaries,
And he will be ready to settle into his new housing accommodation,
It has got to be said,
We all need a friend like him.

Hope

You won't believe me when I say this
But guess what?
Things can get better.
How do I know?"
I don't.
I really don't.
But what do I have that means you can tell me that things will get better.
Well... I have hope.

<u>Let me be</u>

Never did I think this would happen yet again,
I had got through the struggle,
I had already won the battle,
I had already won the war.
Why must it happen again?
Is it a test of my sanity?
A test of my patience?
Surely not.
Surely this was already over.
I was already done.
I will fight this again, but please,
Let me be,
Let me rest.

Pain came back to get me

My legs, floppy and lifeless.
My brain, overactive, intense and harmful.
My back, diligent,
Breaking,
snapping in half.
Intense amounts of pain flowing through my nerves and bones.
I have been through this before,
But this time I feel so torn.

Never did I think that actually me being in pain,
Well, it was me being reborn.
The previous book may have ended,
But we are opening a new.

I learn to dance with my soul,
No matter how much pain I am in.

I learn to sing out louder in the shower,
Even if I am sitting on a bathroom stool.

I learn to love myself,
Despite all the pain,
For if I didn't love myself,
Who would?

Discreet

Discreetly, I think.
I think I'm doing it discreetly.
Unbeknown to me,
You know all about it.
You know about the cuts that lay upon my wrists
You know about the willingness to starve and purge.
You know about the walls I punch with my fists.
The bad words that the voices tell me, they emerge and surge.
The bad thoughts just always seem to lurk.

But now my scars are covered with bright trees and flowers,
For I much prefer the pain of tattoo.
When I head to the bathroom,
I now just shower and take care of myself,
Applying facemasks and moisturising my body,
It no longer feels like such a task.
My walls are covered with positivity,
Positivity to enlighten my soul rather than acting out in frustration.
I had to get used to the voices being so quiet,
So quiet that they are rarely there anymore.

Mental Health Through the Written Word

Mental Illness at its Finest *Trigger Warning*

I get so agitated,
So angry,
So frustrated,
So confused,
So numb,
So God help me.

Help me.
Help me God,
I am begging you,
Please.
Take it away

I am hearing voices,
I am hearing sounds that others' say they aren't there,
Seeing people,
Angels with wings,
Tall men,
Cross legged women with dark dark hair cutting their arms with a kitchen knife,
I couldn't escape the room.
I was stuck.
Stuck in a fucking tomb

I was stuck in a fucking tomb.

Everyone is talking about me,
Laughing at me,
They think I am stupid,
That I am a nuisance
Things are happening that people are saying never happened.
I call you all liars and I feel so lonesome.
Then I see a gorgeous white poodle in my room and I KNOW,
I KNOW that cannot be possible.

Every hour I want to die,
I can't take the lies,
I can't take the cries,
Allow the crashing tides and allow me to rest.

I try so hard to remain strong but something has taken over,
I beg,
Please,
I feel so numb now
Take it away.
Hold on

How to Get Better

How do you get better from mental illness?
Don't be silly, you don't.

But you do learn to manage it.
You learn coping strategies,
You tick off your to-do lists,
You learn distraction,
Meditation,
Radical Acceptance,
You take medication,
You practice yoga,
You go to the gym,
You get coffee with your friends
you complete your college assignment.
And then they say the mental anguish will go away,
But only If you keep resisting the urges,
If only you keep resisting the impulses.
If only you can keep your paranoia at bay.
If only you can make the hallucinations and the voices go away.
You have got this.
Have hope.
Hold on.
If only you can hold on.
Just hold on.

I Want to Feel

I feel flat,
Numb even,
Like a flat tyre,
Numb like ice freezing in between your hands.

I want to feel something.
Anything.

Once upon a time, I would have chosen pain,
But now I decorate bouquets of flowers,
I pick one singular rose bud,
And I hope that it blooms,
Just like me.
I lather my numbness with bubbles and soap,
And now I have hope.

27.05.21

Spiralling down?
Cherish your life,
For life is not at the odds of a game,
It is purely down to choices,
Choices you make.

Take accountability for your decisions,
Do what you will,
Do the wrong thing and you will pay,
You will pay,
You will pay with your life.
Gamble your life or spill the T?
Confess and do what you need to do.

There was once a woman who did no wrong,
But the man saw the darkness,
For he stole and fought and made the conscious decision,
The decision would become a solution,
So is it time to play the game, yet?

Survivor

Anxiety keeps me awake,
Whilst my depression is at bay.
Sometimes it is the other way round,
Yet I still cannot sleep safe and sound.
I am lying in my bed trying to subdue my emotional decay.
It feels like I am failing effortlessly,
Then I realise, as I survive second by second,
I am keeping up the fight to survive,
Despite how tired.
There is no effortless failure,
For I am a 'survivor'.

I care about you

Open up your heart,
Is there something else you are waiting for?
Show me the purest of your core,
I can see that it is torn,
That it is sore.

I want to help you restore,
But you need to feed me more.

Do you need help?
As I can tell you are full of lightness,
But I see you now,
I need to know if this is a masquerade.

If you can't find the words,
Then for hours we will play charades,
I will give you the time until you open up your core.

Just don't keep your secrets lay hidden in the shade,
For you deserve more.

The Tunnel

Many people have suffered through hard times in their lives,
Been in places people often describe it as being in a dark, never-ending tunnel,
A tunnel where they can see no light.
It can take many people a very long time to realise this, through no fault of their own,
So imagine this:

You are making your way through a dark, enclosed tunnel, it smells of sewage waste. You have no food or water, and your body is lacking the nutrients it needs to keep going. You are tired, so very tired. You feel you have been walking this journey for years, perhaps you have. You sit down and rest your head against your needs, trying to regulate your breathing. You find yourself dwelling on the time when you first entered this dark enclosure. You had nothing with you. You felt no comfort, no happiness, had no steadiness but you were given one item. You were given a key.

You never knew why you were given this but you carried it anyway because that was all you had. Nobody else had that key, only you could access it, use it, and find its purpose. What you do not realise is that you are carrying the key to your own success. It is not until you find the value of this key that only you can change the position you are in.

You had to find the ladders leading upwards, you have the key to the trap door. You never knew you had to open it to find the light. Certain things can help you, such as the keys you possess, the people around you. However, only you have the power to create the transition and eventually you will find the light.

Going beyond

Insomnia goes beyond the inability to sleep,
It means late at night,
Your thoughts get too deep,
As you leap to leap between different scenarios and glance through each of your bedroom
Windows.
Insomnia goes beyond the inability to sleep,
Sometimes your eyes begin to leak,
Scared to fall asleep,
Knowing your dreams to be twisted,
Knowing they need to be tweaked.
Insomnia is so desperately needing sleep,
Your eyes are heavy,
You think you are ready.
Ready to sleep now and so you close your eyes,
Only to sigh when you realise two hours later the body is continuing to fight sleep,
like a leopard chasing it's prey.
I need to sleep.
Yet, insomnia goes beyond the inability to fall asleep.

I Listen to my Angels

Anxiety melting within my chest,
My heart stinging from pins and needles,
The sword drawing it out of my chest,
My stomach laid at the bottom of its depths.
This melting pot is too much for me,
The physicality of how it manifests itself is just too much.
Watch me.
Watch me trying to soothe my tangled nerves with hot peppermint tea.
Can you see?
I just want to sleep,
Watch my entire body shake,
As i feel my heart screaming 'beat, beat, beat'.
Please.
Let me sleep.
Watch me,
I can't catch a breath.
Is this what it feels like to die?
My hands are tied.
I am met with an army,
An army of superiors,
Catapulting bullets,
Washing over me like a fatal tsunami.
Nobody knows me,
Nobody knew me.
So, Watch me.
Watch me as my chest enlarges as I gulp for air.
I take a moment, I rest and I cry.
For it feels like I can't sit with this anymore.
Watch me.
Instead, I scream into my cushioned bedding.
I stand up and I fight.
Watch me.
WATCH ME.
I fight for what I know is best.
Put me to do the god damn test.
See me cry,
See me clutch my chest.
Watch me beg to the angels asking and pleading with them, for them to tell me everything
is going to be okay.
But most importantly,
Most significantly,
Watch me stand up.
Watch me as I clutch my chest,
and watch me as I put up a fight.

Resilience

The rain poured down on her,
She took it in her stride,
she continued to fly through the storm.

My Dearest Sister

You grew up too fast,
I knew it wouldn't last.
It was too good to be true,
Now I feel like I'm losing you.
Your skin, your eyes, your soul,
Grey-blue like the sea,
I feel your wisdom,
I feel your soul,
I feel your soul within me,
I see you.
Don't you see?
You're special to me.
You are the motive through and through,
I will wait in line,
Stand in a queue,
Waiting,
Waiting for my time,
For my time to watch you grow.
Just so I know you made it,
So, I know you made it through.
Take my hand my dear,
And we will fly once again,
Ten to the dozen,
You made it through.
You made it through

You are Enough

It's sad, isn't it?
That you see so many people just ready to quit,
Ready to give it all up,
Really gives you that view,
That close-up perspective.
Looking at that drive of willingness to help,
Despite your thoughts mirroring their behaviour.
That close-up,
You realise it is you too.
You're fucked up too.

This time is different,
I will not be ignored,
I will not be belittled,
I will not feel guilty.
I am more than enough.

This world,
This shit,
It Is tough,
No wonder people are ready to give up.

The fact we feel this way,
It's fucked up.
But let's not do this,
Let's choose not to give up.

All we can do is try,
We don't have to lie,
Don't have to lie to ourselves anymore,
Because all of us,
All of us are enough,
Remember that.
You are enough.

Ignoring the Outside World

The whole world is a complete mess,
Yet here I am,
Playing chess.

Marbles

My eyes are clear crystal marbles,
You will never see a tear shed.
I let you all think, I am on the mend,
But at night, the marbles disappear,
I swim in a flood of tears,
Holding the very own marbles that used to be mine,
Weighing me down,
Head under water.
It is sunrise, and my shiny marbles become part of me again,
Never letting you see a tear I may shed.

The light of the Priory

An obscure place like this,
Where the bushes are overgrown,
A foundation of a mounting cliff is made of too many stones
Where the trees are bundled too close together,
And the leaves whisper among themselves,
There is a light.

Somehow in the dark and suppressed energy that drives us to madness,
In the muffling voices we hear at night,
In the sight of horrors that push us further into depths of darkness,
There is a light.

But you know what?
In this atrocity of revulsion,
Where everything seems so dejected and blue,
We have to understand,
There is a light.

For the beings of light who choose to enter such wildnerness,
With barely any profit,
From the goodness of purity that seeps out of their souls,
They help us see light,
There is a light.

It may take a while,
Whether it may be weeks or months,
Whether it will take less stress, more engagement and further reward,
Whether it will take meditation or medication
We will eventually see that light,
There is a light.
My anxiety persists,
Even after everything,
Even after all these drugs.
Yet somehow,
I know I must learn to manage it myself.

They feed me skills of mindfulness,
Suggesting working with my hobbies,
So here I am writing a poem.
A poem to restore my breathing,
A poem to restore my heart.
Allowing the anxiety to flow by,
Just accepting it.
Accepting that I am feeling this way.

Knowing it will pass with time.

Printed in Great Britain
by Amazon